CORNWALL

Edited by Lucy Jenkins

First published in Great Britain in 1999 by
YOUNG WRITERS
Remus House,
Coltsfoot Drive,
Woodston,
Peterborough, PE2 9JX
Telephone (01733) 890066

HB ISBN 0 75431 692 0
SB ISBN 0 75431 693 9

FOREWORD

Young Writers have produced poetry books in conjunction with schools for over eight years; providing a platform for talented young people to shine. This year, the Celebration 2000 collection of regional anthologies were developed with the millennium in mind.

With the nation taking stock of how far we have come, and reflecting on what we want to achieve in the future, our anthologies give a vivid insight into the thoughts and experiences of the younger generation.

We were once again impressed with the quality and attention to detail of every entry received and hope you will enjoy the poems we have decided to feature in *Celebration 2000 Cornwall* for many years to come.

CONTENTS

Mylor Bridge School

Chloe Rogers 83

Nancledra School

Joseph Walker 83
Zac John Birchley 84
Tomas Griffin 85
Elizabeth Birchley 85
Timmy Thompson 86
Harrison Evans 86
Ross Becalick 87
Rosie Chapman 87
Emma Nankervis 88
Matthew King 88
Orlando Bird 89
Lawrence Kennedy 89
Christopher Olds 90
Guthrie Musser 90
Alf Brockett 91

St Ives Junior School, Cornwall

Jacqueline Luckham 92
Emily Rowe 92
James McGovern 93
Daniel Rouncefield 93
Catherine Powell 94
Hannah Rose Rimmer 94

St Merryn School, Padstow

Emily Kessell 95
Bryn Dolman 96
Hollie Cogdale 97
Benjamin Lee Milby 98
Chris Thomas 99
Karl Hughes 100
Clark Mills 101

Treloweth CP School

The Poems

2001

Weird inventions being made,
Computers roaming the mighty wonderful world,
Megabytes wherever I look,
No butlers, computers instead,
Children watching TV all the time,
Horrible robots doing our work,
Computerised houses being built
Over the countryside
Computer chips everywhere I go.

Cheryl Richards (10)
Boskenwyn CP School

I WISH

I hope the computers don't crash,
So we can all have a millennium bash,
I wish the Millennium Dome,
Was to come and fly to my home.
We'll have lots of balloons and cool songs,
And listen to the 12 midnight bongs.

I wonder what will happen
in the future?

Áine Bailey (9)
Boskenwyn CP School

LONELY BEACH

I lie on the deserted beach watching the scarlet sun go down,
A lonely seagull squawks trying to find its long gone friends,
The waves lap lazily, the rhythm drifting me to sleep.
The swaying palms wake me with the drop of a coconut
And I drink the cool, refreshing milk that smoothly slides down my
throat.
The water's creeping slowly nearer wetting my warm toes.
Wait, a child cries in the far distance, silence broken.
My peace is shattered.

Jinny Wadworth (11)
Boskenwyn CP School

BUMBLE THE GUINEA PIG

I'm sitting here watching the quick scamperer,
His small velvet nose twitching.
Beady, brown eyes watching your every move.
He is white with a black bottom,
He's a lettuce muncher,
He has sharp thin claws,
At the end of his tiny, pink legs.

Simoné Foreman (11)
Boskenwyn CP School

GALLOPING AT SPEED

Yes, I remember galloping
With the wind darting by my face
Deafening me with whistling
So loud around the place.

Late February, if I am right,
The weather so cold but dry,
I dreamt of galloping that night,
As the trees went whizzing by.

I smelt the flowers' beautiful scent,
Before I heard the humming bees,
I felt the wind's powers that bent
The poor swaying trees.

Tasting the clear and chilly air,
Feeling I was in paradise,
Gliding around without a care,
Galloping at speed.

Emma-Clare Harriet Rowe (11)
Cardinham CP School

THE DARK MORNING

I woke in cold and darkness.
It was six in the morning.
I could hear the birds in the trees.
I felt coldness shiver through the covers.
I could see nothing but plain, pitch black.
I could see the sun shine through the window.

Michael Logan (11)
Cardinham CP School

MOVING HOUSE

Moving ornaments and cupboards
So fast, so frantic, so quickly.
The glimpse of a moment the finishing touch was made,
And the big smile on Mum's face,
So quick and sudden,
So broad and splendid!
I knew that moment that I would be happy
In that little cottage.

Joe Branston (9)
Cardinham CP School

SNAPSHOTS

I heard a barking dog
and saw a bird flying in the blue and white sky.
It was a robin.

I saw smoke blowing sideways from a chimney.
It was stinking.
A fluffy white cat sat on a roof.
It was asleep.

Michael Jepson (8)
Cardinham CP School

SPRING SONG

There came a day that caught the winter,
Killed it,
Melted it down,
And shaped it into rain.

What shall I do with the rain?
The day said, the day said.
Call the sun
To lap it up

And what shall I do with the clouds?
The day said, the day said,
Wring them out,
Make them white as new born lambs

And what shall I do with the deer?
The day said, the day said.
Put them on high ground,
Let them graze on green grass.

There came a day and he was spring,
His mouth open in astonishment,
A new born lamb black not white,
Being licked off gently by its mother.

Matthew Orton (10)
Cardinham CP School

HAIKU

One stormy cold night
Dark clouds move slowly across
Like a misty road.

Jennifer Mackie (9)
Cardinham CP School

HAIKU

Bright morning sunshine.
Silver waves darting away
Like glistening coins.

Shauna Prideaux (10)
Cardinham CP School

HAIKU

Freezing morning air.
Trees full of cold white wet frost
Like a fake snow scene.

Luke Halton (8)
Cardinham CP School

HAIKU

Colourful morning
With the wind rushing by me
Like the speed of cars.

Rachel Ball (8)
Cardinham CP School

HAIKU

The midday sunshine,
Ocean crashes viciously
Like an angry bear.

Eleanor Jo Devenish (8)
Cardinham CP School

MY FIRST SIGHT OF JED

A cute adorable puppy
Snuggled in a basket of jumpers and blankets.
The best things I remember are . . .
A tuft standing right up
White markings on the tip of his tail and his forehead,
He was as golden as a beach.
Sleeping forever,
Soft as a rabbit.
I smelled that certain doggy smell
That filled me with joy.

Charlotte Heath (9)
Cardinham CP School

RATS

Those people think
I have a long tail,
eyes like cherry tomatoes,
pointed ears, and that
I'm a troublemaker,
food monster,
wall-nibbler,
dusty, dirty, disgusting,
crawling creature.

Morwenna Orton (8)
Cardinham CP School

CELEBRATION 2000
SPACE STATION SILICON VALLEY

The chip that's in the station has brought
about a futuristic age of creation,
The animals that will be there will begin to scream and scare,
especially when the foxes get mad at the bears,
it'll be the bears that are blamed.
The huskies who are stressed will fight the
penguins who are vexed.
The ostriches and the hippos racing all the time,
the hippos and ostriches looking up at all the sights
until they see a bird up in flight.
It's a parrot high up in the gloomy sky.

Nicholas Schenk (10)
Charlestown CP School

CYBER PETS

Cyber pets, Cyber pets they beep all day,
Just as they stop, they start again,
You have to give them injections,
Feed them all day,
And when you've finished you're shouting hooray,
Then you remember to put them to sleep,
You get quite tired,
You go to bed,
You wake up in the morning,
And your Cyber pet's dead,
I press the reset button,
Nothing happens,
It's gone for good!

Edward Johnson (10)
Charlestown CP School

THE POWER OF PLAYSTATION

Nintendos, Amigas everywhere,
Segas and Saturns,
Certainly not rare
But now a new invention,
Caught all of our attention.
It's grey and square,
With technology everywhere.

The Anolog Controller and Rumble Pack,
Never, ever in the tiny bit lack.
Fun and fame with the average game.
The memory card and cool steering wheel,
The multi-tab and luscious light gun,
Have plenty and plenty of fabulous fun.

Tomb Raider 3 and Final Fantasy 7,
Really carry your minds
Into the heavens.
Coolboarders 2 and Tekken 3,
Really mean the world to me.
Metal Gear Solid and Pandemonium 2,
Will really really appeal to you.

The PlayStation still,
Is never a bore,
And will always offer much much more.

Ross Phillips (11)
Charlestown CP School

THE CAT

The cat,
sitting in the window watching
the birds fly by.

      Now the cat is sitting on the grass
      waiting for his moment to strike
      then a little chaffinch lands on
      a branch in front of the cat.

Now the cat is in the house,
with feathers all around,
in comes a lady, looks at the
cat and screams.
For, you see the cat and the bird
are mortal enemies.

      Then in struts the dog
      the cat looks up,
      the dog looks down and smiles.

The cat runs out the door and up a tree.
While the cat is up the tree,
the dog barks violently
but as long as the cat stays
up the tree the dog will never get it.

Callum Jeffery-Payn (10)
Charlestown CP School

THE SPY

Peeping through the bushes,
Glancing in the windows,
Scratching in the notebook.
He needs to find some clues.

The suspect could be anywhere,
Creeping all around,
Following his next victim,
Crouching close to the ground.

Danger in the air,
Heart thumping quickly,
Eagle eyes waiting.
For danger to spot.

Fingers burning like fire,
Hands sweating buckets,
Legs ready to pounce,
And capture the enemy.

Fierce as a tiger,
Yet quiet as a mouse,
Run like a cheetah,
Even if you're as small as a mouse.

When will the struggle start,
We've got no time to waste,
Before the day leaves us,
And greets us with dusk.

Holly Emma Jones (10)
Charlestown CP School

PARTY TIME!

Where are you going?
Or are you staying?
What are you going to do?
I'm going to *celebrate!*

> We're going to a party
> To have some fun!
> To have a makeover
> And look the stylish one!

We're going to a party
At Carlyon Bay Hotel
It's my Gran's big day
She's 2000 here today!

> She's got a new red hat
> It stays on her head
> Until she goes to bed
> She looks like she's
> *Celebrating!*

We made a toast
To another 2000 years
Of peace, harmony
And no new found wars!

> We've got to celebrate
> She's now 2000!
> She's lived in two centuries
> And had four babies.

She's now left us and gone
To find a new life
To live as long.

I will remember my gran
Because she's my 2000 year old nan.

Eliza Amy Rowe-Best (10)
Charlestown CP School

THE FUTURE

What will happen in the future?
What will happen tomorrow?
Will I win a car?
Or will I win a million pounds?
Who knows.

What will happen in two days?
What will happen next week?
Will the bank get robbed?
Or will I get the flu?
Who knows.

What will happen next year?
What will happen in two weeks?
Will I get the Millennium Bug?
Or will we turn into monkeys?
Who knows.

Andrew Sampson (10)
Charlestown CP School

MY PETS

I have got a brown and white furry dog,
He always does a steady jog.
I have got a yellow and blue budgerigar,
When he spreads his wings he looks like a star.

I have got a big goldfish,
He is getting so big he can hardly fit in his dish.
I have got another dog, she is as black as coal,
She is so small she is like a mole.

I used to have a cat called Sueky,
When I stroked her fur she felt so silky.
I used to have another dog, she was called Snoopy,
We had to put her down because she kept having heart attacks.
I wish she could just come back!

Helen Guy (10)
Charlestown CP School

THE CAT'S PARTY

I let my cat out when we were celebrating the year 2000
I shut the door before I saw . . .
Heard . . .
The whole of the town's cats.
They all were dancing.
One cat was playing a tambourine.
Another was playing a sweet violin.
An alley cat was beating a drum with his fat tum.
A Siamese was tiptoeing across a plank.
My cat was swaying and doing a back flip.
There was a brown mouse with a sparkling hat.

Who looked to be part of the act.
To tell you the truth I think he was a DJ.
All the cats were swaying to the music.
They didn't notice that I was there.
Some cats got up onto their back paws
And scooted along the front alley walls.
An acrobat was doing an act with a cat.
A cat fell down and after that another.
I heard someone say 'It's raining cats out there.'

Michelle Murray (10)
Charlestown CP School

PARTY TIME

10, 9, 8, 7, 6, 5, 4, 3, 2, 1, Here comes the millennium.
Everyone's jumping with joy,
Screaming and shouting, the millennium is here,
The streets light up,
The doors all open,
Then they shout 'The millennium is all about.'

Up and down the streets they run,
People dancing everywhere.
Fireworks in the sky,
Even pets watching,
Dogs barking, cats crying,
The party still goes on,
People chanting millennium,
Bottles of champagne going pop,
It's the early hours of the morning,
Many people are still partying
But I'm tucked up in bed!

Rachael Smith (10)
Charlestown CP School

THE YEAR 2000

5, 4, 3, 2, 1, millennium!
It's here, the year,
The year 2000!
Everyone's partying,
Everyone's cool,
The streets light up
Everyone's out, and they shout,
It's the millennium, and it's all about!

> Everyone's dancing,
> Everyone's shouting
> 'Millennium! The year 2000!'
> 'It's here! It's here!'
> 'Champagne all around!'
> 'To the millennium!' They cry.

Natalie Sullivan (10)
Charlestown CP School

EVERYONE CELEBRATES 2000

Let's all have a celebration,
Everyone in the nation,
The year 2000 will be here,
'Partytime' we all cheer.

Let's have a disco,
Where everyone can go,
Dancing to our favourite song,
Rocking and rolling all night long.

Let's have a party in the street,
Lots of people to meet and greet,
Food and drink for everyone,
Come along it will be fun.

Fireworks to light the sky,
Beautiful as they rise up high,
Bangers banging very loud,
Frightening the crowd.

A holiday would be fun,
Especially in the sun,
I will save all my money,
To go on holiday with daddy and mummy.

Disneyland is my dream,
See Mickey Mouse and his team,
What a way to celebrate,
The year 2000 will be great.

Hannah Retallick (11)
Charlestown CP School

THE LION

The lion is big,
And has quite dark coloured fur.
He's the King of the jungle,
And has animals all around him to praise him,
The lion is a member of the cat family.
He catches his prey between his paws,
He pounces round and round all day long
And roars very loud,
He has razor sharp teeth,
He has a mane around his face,
And a tuft on the end of his tail.
He eats lots of animals,
He has nice long whiskers on his face
And has a pinkish nose,
The lion is a great animal with sharp claws.

Becky A Slater (10)
Charlestown CP School

CELEBRATION 2000 PARTY

You can dance to music.
Sing some songs.
It's nearly 2000
And it's time to party, all night long.

> You're going to look glamorous.
> You're going to be the best one there,
> So stylish! so cool! are you going to a ball?
> Yes, I am I'm going to the 2000 ball with my best
> friend Chloe Light.

I bought a new dress,
It cost me a bomb!
But wait till you see it.
Cos I look so cool.

> I got a new hair style
> And my nails filed.
> A makeover that made me quite
> tired.

We're staying in a hotel or it could be a motel?
I don't know.
I painted my nails silver
And walked down to the river to meet my friend there.

> It's time to party!
> It's 2000!
> It's time to celebrate!

Kerry Beynon (10)
Charlestown CP School

THE DRAGON

As the dim and fading light
Struggles to push its way through the thick foliage,
The animals of the day retire to damp holes in the ground
And the long hanging shadows of aged trees,
Undisturbed tranquillity falls over the sharp, icy points of plants,
And the layers upon layers of snow.
The untrodden ground of a dark forbidding cave,
With remains of past victims waits . . . patiently.
Suddenly, without any hesitation, a spine-tingling groan
Echoes around the cave;
A sharp gust of wind is followed by a shower of rocks.
Scattered effortlessly out of the black abyss.
Just as the hand of dusk grips firmly on the landscape,
A great beast plunders out, fresh from hibernation.
The silhouette of the admirable creature flings its head,
And lets rip an enormous jet of flames
That meander meaninglessly off into the atmosphere.
The animal with the talent of literally every living soul on the
planet,
Licks its razor sharp claws, which could tear even the toughest of
hinds,
And straightens out its patterned wings.
With immense power it hauls itself into the air,
leaving behind only heavy deep footprints.
The heat seeking animal takes a long journey upwards,
and nestles contentedly in the sun.

William Best (11)
Charlestown CP School

TIGER

Tiger, tiger, where are you now?
Hiding in the long, thick grass
Or in a big canyon - the cause for a big stampede?
Hungry for food-screaming for food
Darkness falls and you still haven't caught anything.
Maybe you will catch food in the morning.
Morning has come another chance to catch some food.
Antelope nearby chomping at the grass,
Flamingos flying in the air above your head.
Behind there are two pythons fighting over a mouse.
Tiger, tiger, are you going to jump high for flamingo?
Or run up fast to catch an antelope?
Seconds later, the tiger runs and stops;
Looking for a hiding place before she pounces.
She's found it.
Minutes, seconds go past and there she goes,
Running all around to find the weakest antelope.
She has caught it, it is succulent and juicy.
Tiger, tiger you found food today -
But will you find food tomorrow?
We will all wonder.

Joanna Hume (11)
Charlestown CP School

THE RALLY DRIVER

When I turn the key
And the engine revs up,
When I just escape death,
After hitting a tree,
When I skid on the mud
And just miss the crowd,
Did you ever realise that I am so proud?

I went around the course at one hundred and twenty,
Missed a reindeer - then spun out on a bend.
I was going along at one hundred and forty -
Smashed into an opponent; he skidded out!
I shot through the finish line grinning gleefully -
Went out of control praying pleafully!
I dodged a cat then hit a cow,
I crashed into the forest - I don't know how!
When I am rallying, I want to be the best,
Now I know I am just a pest.

The last time I rallied,
I killed a spectator,
My rallying days are over
I am due in court later.
After all the things I've said and done,
I might as well take up Formula 1!

Louis Rolfe (11)
Charlestown CP School

MY BIKE

I have got a bike,
It's pale blue with a big, shiny light,
I can ride it at night,
Most people don't care
They just watch me and stare,

At my lovely new pale blue bike.

My old bike was nasty,
It was very old and rusty,
And I couldn't stand the light,
It just wasn't right.
The wheels were worn out,
It just didn't feel right
Riding along on that bike.
My new bike is special,
It is very shiny and smooth,
It has ten special grooves.

All my friends are jealous.
Of my lovely new, pale blue bike.

Rebecca White (11)
Charlestown CP School

ENDANGERED ANIMALS

Disappearing all the time,
Elephants, Squirrels, Pandas,
And that's not all.
People hunt them for their tusks,
Make them into medicine,
That's only the elephants,
Pandas' fur made into rugs,
Deers' antlers for ornaments,
Hunt them!
Shoot them!
Catch them!
Trap them!
Chase them!
That's not all;
They rip them to pieces,
Or stuff them for show.
Poor Animals.
Protect them,
Please.

Gemma Morcom (11)
Charlestown CP School

THE DREADED TV

Everyone likes Mr DiCaprio,
While most toddlers like Po.
Most people like watching TV,
While resting both knobbly knees.
New programmes have come on the screen,
While horror films make us scream!
Children's programmes teach ABCs
And Winnie the Pooh likes honeybees.
Some people like comedy with Dawn French,
In the vicar of Dibley she sits praying on a bench.
Mums and Dads watch Songs of Praise,
While children are really crazed,
By Adidas, Reebok- what is next?
Some comedians make me laugh,
But some of the jokes are really daft.
Most children like at least one soap,
With Peggys and Grants that gloat.
They always have dramatic text,
Oh what will TV bring next?!

Bethany Jones (11)
Charlestown CP School

HAMSTER TROUBLE

Nibbling on its favourite food,
But when it has all gone,
He gets into a mood!
He wants much more,
He calls the law,
But I don't know what he wants.
He bites my finger,
It really hurts,
But then he has lots of burps!
Plodding along on the sawdust of his cage,
Getting in a right bad rage,
Sitting on my lap,
Nibbling at my jumper,
I call him a little monster!
He escapes the next day
And I check under
The sofa
Behind the fireplace,
And out in the hall.
Out in the kitchen then out in the garden,
I can't find him anywhere!
I check in the cage again,
And there I see him laughing at me.
Nibbling on a biscuit crumb.
I know he won't get any rest from me!

Kirsty Beach (11)
Charlestown CP School

NAUGHTY BROTHERS AND SISTERS

How annoying, shouting and screaming when you just hit him
with a spoon.
My sister gets so angry that she wallops me with a broom.
The pets are all dead from a bonk on the head,
Who are now buried under the garden shed.
We have lost our cat - no guesses where it is.
With all the junk in my brother's room.
It seems like that I am the only sane child in the house.
My sister keeps a mouse in a cardboard box,
Which escapes every day.
There are lots of times when I am in a daze
Thinking about lazing on a lovely hot beach.
Away from my brother and away from my sister
Oh what bliss!
My brother was climbing a tree,
Got stung by a bee,
Fell on his head,
Concussed himself to death.
Then I woke up,
It was all a dream.
I scream and I scream.

Charlotte Frances Barnes (11)
Charlestown CP School

TEACHER TROUBLE 2000

Has your teacher ever annoyed you?
Has she ordered you around?
Has she made you clean the blackboard?
I bet she's made you sweep the ground?
Teachers always pick on someone
In your case, it's always you
She makes you pick up crumbs at lunchtime
And clean out the staffroom loo!
Teachers nowadays get answers from a handbook
And when a child is stuck they just take a look
And then they pretend they know every answer
And make you call them madame or master
And when breaktime comes they retire to the staffroom
Pretending they've been working all day
They sit down in a chair for some biscuits and tea
While we're freezing out at play
And as for the homework, she gives you too much
You struggle and strain to start up your brain
To find all the answers for such . . . .
Hard sums and questions for English
They are too hard for you
Because you weren't listening
You were tying your shoe.

Jenny Pyle (11)
Charlestown CP School

THE CAT

Prowling, purring deeply. Gentle paws touch the grass.
She crouches then slowly springs and pounces.
Landing on her agile legs,
She balances before her owner shouts
'Mags! Come here darling. Don't be naughty,
                          what were you trying to do?'
She runs inside and hides behind a shoe.
The owner looks and hesitates. Then walks out the room to fetch
a brush to give the cat a groom.
All is dark, the cat emerges; creeping through the old cat flap.
She runs outside and starts to purr.
Finally free,
It's a dream.
Ducking under the wooden fence.
She escapes in a land free to hunt.
Free from the owner and free from the dog.
She starts to sprint with her long, thin legs.
She crouches low,
then pounces on her prey!

Leach Hunkin (11)
Charlestown CP School

20TH CENTURY FOX

20th Century Fox,
Come out of your box.
What can you see,
My foxy, foxy?

In 1912 Titanic went down,
Help everybody before they drown.
In 1939 World War II broke out,
We played with Hitler, a lethal bout.
In 1945 the war did end,
England we need no longer defend.
In the 70's pop music came onto the scene,
Now it's more popular than it has ever been.
Now it's the 90's computers people mend,
But this decade - it's coming to an end.
The 21st Century is looming too close,
'I've lived to see it!'
The people do boast.

20th Century Fox,
Come out of your box,
What can you see,
My foxy foxy?

I can see
The 21st Century.

Vicky Julian (11)
Charlestown CP School

MY FIRST RED

I was late,
I picked up my boots and ran, ran
like the wind
My jacket slowed me down
I got there in time
Heart thumping
I walked on to the pitch
The crowd roared
I kicked around the ball
Then we started
They took centre
The game began with a buzz
We made a break through
And scored
I took someone out
The ref showed the red
I walked down the tunnel
Disappointed
I took an early bath
I couldn't believe it
My first red.
My Manager said 'It won't be your
last my son.'

Gary Bone (11)
Charlestown CP School

FOOTBALL FANTASY

Football, football, brilliant football.
3 o'clock, 12 o'clock, 8 o'clock, 9 o'clock.
Manchester United 20 - Liverpool 0.
Coventry 19 - Arsenal 1.
When the final whistle goes - what a rush!
The managers often are happy and often are sad.
Man Utd rule.
Andy Cole is cool.
England's trip to France.
Was never worth the entrance.
I went to Wembley.
It is still stuck in my memory.
I have never been to Old Trafford.
I have also never been to Stratford End.
Football Fantasy, Football Fantasy.
What a brilliant game!
Some footballers feel shame,
What a brilliant night.
For Everton and their might.
A brilliant trier is every man's desire.
Marc Overmars is flying over mars
The Ref showed red to Seaman, looking like a Demon.
Brilliant Football. Brilliant Football.

Chris Daly (11)
Charlestown CP School

WINTER TREES

Shadows looming in the distance,
A lifeless skeleton,
Plain but spooky, dark and lifeless,
That is a winter tree.

An angular framework, dismal colours
A dim spiky tower
Its greenness taken by the fall of winter
but that, in time, will pass.

A silhouette against the black and orange skyline,
Making its mark on the face of the earth,
Hundreds of jet black frames, with an evil air
around them,
Waiting for summer's red fire.

Ben Phillips (9)
Gorran CP School

DREAMTIME

My dreamtime box is full of -
Everchanging weather that brings us
wetness and warmth.
Mountains standing straight and tall,
Stars glistening full of brightness,
Water coming through springs in the mountains,
Plants growing upwards higher and higher,
Birds singing softly and sweetly,
yummy food that keeps me alive,
Forests of tall trees and squelching mud,
The beautiful moon that shines all night,
Animals running into the distance ....

Amanda Deakin (9)
Gorran CP School

Looking Through The Window Of 1999 I Gaze At . . .

The pollution of the world
Dirty factories poisoning the people and the air.
Acid rain infecting the trees with its little
Drops of lemon juice.

I observe homeless people filled with fear,
A pile of boxes no use any more.
A tree's leaves sad, hungry and hopeless.
Thirsty and cold with rags and nowhere to
Go, just skin and bones.

I witness children and adults starving thirsty and hungry.
Crying, suffering and dying.
A hopeless pile battered and bored.

I note teenagers being foolish with drugs,
Irresponsible people overdose on ecstasy
Swallowing heroin unhappy and foolish.

Alice Sibley (10)
Gorran CP School

Dreamtime

The ancient creaking of trees
The spark from flint tipped rock
The stone churning sea
The spear tipped grass
The stony soil waiting to be ploughed
The setting of the summer sun.

Chris de Courcy (10)
Gorran CP School

LOOK THROUGH THE WINDOW OF 1999

Looking through the window of 1999.
I saw teenagers taking drugs dizzy, sick and injecting themselves.

I stared at homeless people begging for food and money,
tramps screaming 'Help me, please help me I'm dying.'

I glimpsed at starving people in Africa, like
a lifeless tree with lost souls.

Opening the door to the new millennium
I wish that the children in Africa will have full tummies.

I hope that people will stop taking drugs and to have a happy life.

I would like all the homeless people to have a peaceful life.

I want all the criminals to stop ruining people's lives.

Harriet Burt (11)
Gorran CP School

DREAMS

The scent of roses; sweet and musical
The glow of meadows; warm and welcoming,
The glittering sun; laughing and joyful.
The playing stars; winking and blinking,
The tall, proud mountains; big and snooty.
The crashing waves; knowing and deciding
The big, white moon; wise and old.
The splashing rain; pittering and pattering
The kindness of the world; spreading joy.
The light of the world; elegant and beautiful.

Chloe Dennis (11)
Gorran CP School

LOOKING THROUGH THE WINDOW OF 1999

I see an evil gangster, greedy and selfish,
Teenagers kidnapping, people are filled with fear,
Thieves being selfish.
I look at starvation, a lifeless tree that has lost its leaves,
Dirty torn rags, people hungry and thirsty.
Children crying whilst trying to get to sleep.
Disease spreading and people suffering.
I notice people with drugs in their pocket,
Teenagers irresponsibly injecting, swallowing pills, sniffing glue,
Angry, elated, unhappy, crying to themselves.
I witness war in the world, battle to the death.
Soldiers attacking with guns, bombs exploding
Competition taking over.
I observe homeless people
Starving with no food to eat and no water to drink.
Poor and ill, battered and bruised,
Crying sad and lonely.

Opening the door to the millennium

I would like crime of the world to exist no more.
People building up confidence.
People's tummies begin to fill up, as starvation of the world vanishes.
Drugs no longer sit in people's pockets as they live happy normal lives.
The war of the worlds is extinct.
People live in a peaceful world.
Homeless people now have homes,
Happy with lots of friends.

Danielle Bray-Smith (9)
Gorran CP School

VICTORIAN RAP

In the days of Victoria the Queen
many changes were to be seen.
Queen for almost sixty-four years
People had such awful fears
death of children that suffer from diseases
people picking up soft wool pieces.

In the days of Victoria the Queen
many changes were to be seen.
Mouldy food that poor have to eat
lots of people living on the street.
Rags for clothes that people wear
life then just wasn't fair.

Sophie Meramveliotaki (9)
Gorran CP School

SPACE WAS WEIRD!

Space cold and empty
No one came to play
I was there all alone
Scared I would die
Getting into my craft
Suddenly I began to cry
Then *whoosh* I started to fly
Dozy, dreaming
Zero thought went into my head
Space was great on my first day.
My thoughts were wrong,
That's what I'd say.

Imogene Steed (11)
Gulval CP School

SPACE

Shhh! Woosh! Blast-Off!
The space ship's zooming up,
It's racing through space past the moon
Flying past stars and planets,
Going through asteroids,
Flying past hot planets and comets.
Zooming up faster than the speed of light.
Woosh!

Going slowly past an eerie, cold isolated planet
With a light, sharp, blue sky,
With a huge silvery star.
Mountains cold and bare stick up from the ground,
With a huge dip right in the middle.

Now we're zooming past Saturn with its asteroids,
Forming a huge ring.
Slowing again past Pluto with ice mountains
Frozen floors.
Zooming to Jupiter with its hot floors
And one huge spot like an eye.
We're on our way back now.

We're back at the moon,
Earth is in sight.
We're gliding down to Earth,
Woosh!

Jake Kimber (10)
Gulval CP School

SPACE

I am on my way in a spaceship
racing through space at a million miles an hour
twinkling stars, flashing comets
it was cold
flashing hot
rumbling noises and bright sparks.

A rocky surface
I am in my suit bobbing up, down
I felt real
I felt like I have never walked before
gliding around
It is such fun.

Icy cold and freezing
there are icicles
dark, damp, rocky and lit up
I went to see the satellite
Wow!

I am on way back in a spaceship
racing through space at a million miles an hour
twinkling stars,
flashing comets,
it was odd,
flashing hot,
rumbling noises, and bright sparks.

Tamsyn Goody (10)
Gulval CP School

SPACE

Racing with time
The stars flashing past
As we fly weightless up, up, up
The bleak landscape absent of its wind
The skywalking sky then dust again, again, again
Rock piled upon another and another
The flying background
As we bounce free with space.

I was in that world once
Where nothing mattered, you were free to roam
It was a new experience as if my body had left me
I was there once in that new world.

Hannah Reid (9)
Gulval CP School

SPACE

Travelling alone in complete silence.
Icy, damp and hollow
there were quiet whispery noises.
Beep! Beep! Beep!
The spaceship alarms went off
Oh no, we are running out of oxygen
Quick put another tank in.
Phew that's over!
Let's go and explore.
Stars running past me
Running, running, running away.
Neptune is massive
　　　　Wow!
Stars running, running, running away.

Ilona Cloke (10)
Gulval CP School

UNTITLED

I'm flying in a spaceship all day and night
it's cool at first but then it's not much might.
It's cold, draughty,
you can't play and you cannot hear a thing.
It's lonely everywhere and I'm chilled right to my bones
but when the rocks crash and go *Boom!*
the space rattles inside me,
it's very frightening.
The planets are silent but in my heart I feel something watching me
but then I see a spaceship going past.
I say help me but there in the window
there was a dead body
and I saw a hideous creature
coming, but it was saying help me,
and I said 'What from?' Then it said from the JGZO
it's big and strong, then it was coming. I said
'*Help* goodbye' and ran back to the spaceship
but it was gone and I sang a song, a song.
Then an alien came to me and said 'Come here' and I did
Then he said your spaceship was at the sun, burnt
then the alien took me back to Earth.

John Davies (10)
Gulval CP School

UNTITLED

Icy gasses floating all around
Saturn in the distance icy
Gassy rings around Saturn
Sun goes down
Saturn all alone except for stars
That look like broken glass.

Devan Blake (10)
Gulval CP School

SPACE

Millions of bare icy stars
Illuminated by sub-tropical storms,
Desolate realms of burning volcanoes
Exploding with lava and crimson fire,
Regions of snow-capped, frosty mountains
Raging atmospheres with a temperature of zero.

Desolate realms of burning volcanoes
Exploding with lava and crimson fire,
Millions of bare icy stars
Illuminated by sub-tropical storms,
Raging atmospheres with a temperature of zero
Regions of snow-capped frosty mountains.

Regions of snow-capped, frosty mountains
Raging atmospheres with a temperature of zero,
Millions of bare icy stars
Illuminated by sub-tropical storms,
Desolate realms of burning volcanoes
Exploding with lava and crimson fire.

Jordan Butler (11)
Gulval CP School

SPACE

Here up in space it's absolutely still
It's lonely and icy, to the bone comes a chill.
Up in the sky is a star.
It's a pity it's ever so far.
It glows like a rose,
It flows as it shows,
If only it wasn't so far.

Charlie Rorke (11)
Gulval CP School

UNTITLED

Racing through the jet stream winds of Jupiter,
Only glancing at the Earth of the future,
Then at the Nepture of the past.
The red fire of the Mars volcanoes,
Turned down by the beauty of Saturn's rings.
Venus with its fiery flare surrounds the jet black void,
Before frazzling all beings in temperatures beyond imagination.
Pluto with its frozen moon creates a sudden loneliness,
While the never-ending flight of Mercury dazzles everything.
Uranus has the glory task of wonder,
But Earth has life,
Earth has enough for everything on it.

Adam Gunderson (9)
Gulval CP School

SPACE

The ice has fallen
The planet is bare
Lonely, barren . . . and shiveringly cold.
The rings are transghostly
The sky is full . . .
Full of stars.

Volcanic eruptions
And winds swirling round at a trillion miles an hour
Geysers bubbling hot with a ghostly mist.

A storm is brewing
And clouds are massing
Hiding the planet
From the view of man.

Cyrus Mills (11)
Gulval CP School

LONELY

Planets whizzed past
Pluto, Venus and Neptune
New planets also
whizzed by.

Saturn's beautiful rings,
and the eerie,
looking moon.
Its icy surface,
so lonely looking.

The comet tails
whizzing by,
Racing around space
getting much faster,
by the second.

Jennifer White (10)
Gulval CP School

MY MISTY MORNING

The harbour walls were draped with
seaweed and fishermen's nets.
Mist wraps itself around us like a
Silver blanket.
The rain clings to us in little droplets.
The clouds are like black cotton wool.
Birds float on warm air currents.
Tiny silver ripples are ruffled by the wind,
Boats are huddled close together to keep the wind at bay.

Jessica Gray (10)
Heamoor CP School

A Day At Newlyn Harbour

Working people struggle
In wind and speckled rain.
As the mist hides from your eyes
Something in the hilltops.
Seagulls screech and swoop.

Boats rock from side to side
In the dead, murky ocean.
All clustered against the wall -
Chains so heavy and dull.
The chatter of children.

A forgotten flag flaps
On a tall, rusty mast.
Oil collects in the misty air.

The sun sets in the sky.
The chatter of children fade away
Beyond, beyond . . . . . .

Jade Sara Pryor (10)
Heamoor CP School

Trapped Behind The Harbour Walls

Behind the harbour walls the boats are moored
Like captives,
In a big prison.
Trapped for the moment.
Protected by the harbour wall,
Only to come out at night,
When their master tells them to.
Finally when they return to the harbour.
They are captives once more.

Darren Gall (10)
Heamoor CP School

Wet Newlyn Day

The clouds as black as a night sky
And the sea with ripples like long road bumps.

The water merging with sky to make one,
While the houses stand tall on the hillside.

The shatter of engines as the boats rattle into the harbour.
The wind blowing against the sails giving the boat speed
as it moves.
Darkness under the pier side,
Where shipwrecked boats lie there sound asleep.

Sparks from welders flash in the distance,
Water drops splash from a sagging rope,
To make rings of ripples in the oily water,
Small crates stacked on deck, smelling of fish and
seaweed.

Todd Phillips (11)
Heamoor CP School

Birds

Seagulls eyeing up fishermens' dinners
Waiting in line on mossy green roofs.
Scavenging for fish like vultures,
Battling with the mighty wind.

The turnstone stands on front of the boat
Like a mascot.
It moves its feet like a helicopter blade -
Wandering around like it is looking for
Something.

Aidan Moffatt (11)
Heamoor CP School

THE HUNT

Strong ropes stretch then fall like flexing reins
Straining to hold the tethered boats at rest.
Their wooden flanks rub up against the harbour wall
Their beams reach up as if they have surrendered . . .
But still they buck and struggle to be free.
Sleepy fishermen carry wet nets onto their bound
Boats in the morning air.
Their prisoners are helpless until they loose the ropes.
The masters start the panting engine and begin their hunt.
Like riders on horseback, the nets are now their hounds.
The pack of hunters leave the stable.

Jason Phipps (11)
Heamoor CP School

A NEWLYN DAY

The rain comes down -
Car wipers going to and fro.
Seagulls screaming on the roof tops -
But I tell you tomorrow will be hot.

People looking for their house keys -
People on the beach playing with dogs.
The boats on the beach are full of water
But I tell you tomorrow will be hot.

The rain there came more
Travellers gazing through shop windows
The fish stay in groups for warmth.

Tom Adams (11)
Heamoor CP School

A Rainy Day Down On The Harbour

Misty, dark and damp,
Children in a cramp,
They are getting spoilt,
Smell of smelly fish gas and oil.

Boats are crowded like,
Sheep in a pen,
Birds are swooping over the,
Dark green sea.

There's big boats, small boats,
There's old boats and new boats,
Workmen going past with hair,
That looks like spiders' webs.

Water was dripping from the tops,
Of buildings, there are,
Ropes and wires, nets and bolts,
And children wearing caps.

Only water fishermen catch fish,
Loads of machines ladders and walls,
Rocks and pools.

Rebecca-Jane Wheeler (10)
Heamoor CP School

A Moment In Newlyn

I lean against the rusty rail,
Boats shiver in the harbour,
Weary fisherman battle with the weather.
Dead fish are scattered everywhere,
An eerie sound hovers in the mist.

Matthew Uren (10)
Heamoor CP School

NEWLYN NOISES

Bright orange starfish tangled in green fishy nets.
Seagulls swooping for scraps.
Black fish grouping in green water.
Seagulls swooping for scraps
And fishermen battle against big waves.
Seagulls swooping for scraps.
Limpets solid on the wall of the harbour
Seagulls swooping for scraps.

Merlin Defilippo (10)
Heamoor CP School

WRITING IN THE RAIN

The weather is grey and miserable,
Misty with a spitting of rain.
As I try to write,
Words disappear on the page.
Inky splodges splattering on wet paper.
My book becomes torn and muddy,
As I drop it amongst the boats.

Xanthe Howard (10)
Heamoor CP School

A RAINY DAY AT NEWLYN

Rainy and wet horrible weather,
Boats coming in overflowing with fish and rain on
their decks,
Smelly, oily water,
Grey, misty skies,
And seagulls swooping through the rain.

Tiny fish darting around in the murky waters,
Swimming away from diving gulls,
And colourful oil,
They swim in as the tide slowly comes in,
And shelter under the pier from screeching gulls.

Richard Adams (11)
Heamoor CP School

A NORMAL DAY IN NEWLYN

Splintering rain sprinkled down.
Each boat brings its own wedge
Of parallel ripples, drifting among the
Shivering reflections.

The translucent mist covers the landscape,
Like a worn out blanket.
Boats are rusting from the sea salt, and decks are damp.
The battered boats bob up and down repeatedly.

The whole harbour smells like a welder's workshop.
Birds skim the water.
The welder's sparks brighten the harbour wall.
Boats supply the market with fish.

The big boats bob and the flexible flags flap.
Reflections shiver.
Pigeons perch on the beams of the fish market.
The caught fish are stacked up in crates.

The boats come in, the fish are landed.
Forklifts rumble around, the light on top flashes.
Lorries beep, children chatter.
Fishermen work, and vehicles clatter.

Natalie Collins (10)
Heamoor CP School

COLD AND BARE

Wet, misty, cold and bare.
There was no one there
Only the sounds of clanging metal.
The rubbish flies like torn off petals
The boats huddle
Metal in a muddle.
Welders weld the metal so disformed
The men they mourned.
The weather, so mean and clawed
The monstrous machines so bold
What stories of old sea men can be told.

Darren Keast (10)
Heamoor CP School

MY MORNING DRAPES

The tired tide creeps in silently
Stirring rusty boats from their slumber.
Cold air skims cheeks of shivering children.
Smears of confused oil in the smooth sea.
Black, flapping flags on top of the old boat,
Tangled and tied up ropes cover the deck.
Drops of cold rain bend in swaying water
Developing small ripples.

Jade Hobson (10)
Heamoor CP School

A Misty Day At Newlyn Harbour

Grey skies and misty rain,
Clouds building up,
Rusty boats huddled together,
Trying to keep warm.

Puddles amongst the cobbles,
Soak our shoes,
Seagulls screech and swoop,
Wind ripples the water.

Oil floats on the surface,
In rainbow colours,
A breeze rushing past our faces,
Making our hair fly about.

Jodie Outram (10)
Heamoor CP School

My Newlyn Day

The winds coldness brushes against my face
Boats crawl away into the grey blanket of mist
The screeching and screaming of swooping birds
Raindrops fall onto the green and blue water like bombs
The engine of a boat is like a helicopter
Dead fish lay on the water's bed
Steam flies out of a boat's funnel
The long splutter of engines come from a small boat
The boats move gracefully along the harbour.

Chris Gall (11)
Heamoor CP School

HARBOUR POEM

Disgusting misty weather in the distant view
Fishing boats coming in and unloading.

Roaring sea, calm in the harbour
Rain spitting, sun trying to burst out
Little mackerel lying in the ice, dead.
Rushing vehicles, oil tankers and forklifts
St Michael's Mount in the misty distance
Smooth rippling water
Plenty of boats, most at rest
In the lovely view.

Alistair Sedgeman (10)
Heamoor CP School

NEWLYN HARBOUR

It was wet, cold and misty,
Boats disappear into the mist,
Seagulls twirling in the sky,
Then diving for fish and chips.
Ripples made by very strong winds,
Flags whipping in the low dull sky.
Nets and ropes tangled on boats.
Fish bubbling in the sea,
Lots of fish scattered on a box.
We come to the end of a
Day at Newlyn Harbour.

Charlie White (10)
Heamoor CP School

An Overcast Day

Rain spitting and a little mist.
Boats move inches when waves touch.
Oily rainbow makes soft shapes on the water.
Birds, a whole community of them all in a group by the water.
Harbour walls grey and dull in its way,
Creatures in the depths below scutter to their homes,
Fish squirming around trying to find the surface of life,
Grey cloud forms rain from above,
The rope gently rots away into dust
It has to be replaced one day
In the wind a flag flaps ferociously

The shiver of a ripple drives into the evening sea.
A boat gently glides into the harbour,
Where it lays for the morning to come.

Leoni Hall (10)
Heamoor CP School

I Am A Bubble

I am floating high in the sky.
Up I soar,
Drifting with other bubbles.
I am like a rainbow gliding through
The sky, up so high.
To and fro, around the world.
Dancing through the trees.
I am yellow, green and red,
I am as fat as can be.
Jumping through the air.

Thomas Lyle (8)
Launceston CP School

THE SEA TRIP

The sun was shining brightly
On our day trip to the sea,
We put on our swimming costumes
Our instructor was a he.

We raced across the ocean
To an island far away,
There was a beach we could play on
It was fun I felt so gay.

The next day it was breezy
Tried to get in the dinghy,
The waves were too strong to go out.
My feet were cold and tingly.

We spent all our day playing,
It was time to go to sleep.
There were funny noises at night
So instead I counted sheep.

We got dressed in the morning
Teacher said time to go home.
All the children got in the dinghy
I had lost my very best comb.

But I could buy another,
My instructor said hurry
Because we were about to go,
I got home and had curry.

Leanne Burtonwood (10)
Launceston CP School

THE SEA TRIP

I wake up feeling glad,
I never feel very sad.
I'm going out today,
Swimming with dolphins and to play.

Water all around me.
I dive in the deep blue sea.
They're coming faster look.
Their fins look like a big hook.

They're calling very loud,
A thunder storm in the clouds,
Their sleeky grey tails
Wow! Look at that great big male.

A baby by my side,
Hey look I'm hitching a ride.
Speeding across the bay,
Look out there's a stingray.

Look over there it's dark
Ahh! Help there's a great big shark
The dolphins were playing,
Like the trees which were swaying.

I wake up feeling glad,
I never feel very sad.
I'm going out today,
Swam with dolphins and played.

Alexandra Harris (9)
Launceston CP School

THE SEA TRIP

See the fish swimming wide,
Crawling crabs near the tide,
Dolphins jump close to me,
Splishing, splashing, in the sea.

I saw a lobster big and red,
At the bottom of the sea bed,
Then I saw a long green eel,
Slithering across an old ship's wheel.

See the long silky shark,
Swimming deeply in the dark,
Grinning teeth stare at me,
Let's come again, please . . . let it be.

See the fish swimming wide,
Crawling crabs near the tide,
Dolphins jump close to me,
Splishing, splashing in the sea.

Lyndsey Williams (10)
Launceston CP School

THE SEA TRIP

Hear the waves crashing upon jagged cliffs,
While the gusty winds blow on the soft sands.
As it blows its mighty blow, the sand shifts.
The vicious waves destroy the rock, it falls, *splash!*

The lighthouse flashes to warn the sailors ship.
A ship gets thrown about like a rag doll.
Or otherwise the ship will take a long dip.
There are a lot of ships under the deep sea.

The morning is bright and so is the sea now,
Like the great big ball of flame in the sky.
The captain looks out over the bow.
The ship is sinking like a stone brick, goodbye.

Hear the waves crashing upon jagged cliffs,
While the gusty winds blow on the soft sands.
As it blows its mighty blow, the sand shifts.
The vicious waves destroy the rock, it falls, *splash!*

Daniel Prout (10)
Launceston CP School

UP AND DOWN AGAIN

I secure the rope into my crab
In the holes I place my foot
Up the jagged boulders I go
I pull myself up the cliff,
Feeling weary sitting down to wait until my turn
The big absail awaits
I walk across the uneven rock,
Attach the rope to my dazzling crab
Not scared anymore
Leaning over the granite edge
I start to waddle down
Letting the rope slide through the glove
I leap then stumble push myself back up
Carry on and bound off the rock
Down and down I go
As soon as I know it I'm at the bottom
Breathing rapidly full of joy.

Matthew Downing (10)
Launceston CP School

ROCK CLIMBING

You feel the wind pushing you side to side
And the cold touch of it on your face.
Confident at first
Step to the bottom of the cliff.
They shout 'Below!'
The rope comes spinning down.
Alas you feel afraid.
'Climbing!' you shout.
Up you go.
'Don't look down!' they shout up to you.
You hear how far below they really are.
To the top at last
You are safe.
'What is next?' you say,
With a smile on your face.

Matzen O'Neill (9)
Launceston CP School

THE SEA TRIP

The boat was out at sea.
In the dead of night.
All was serene and still.

Mist was blocking their eyes
From the dark came sighs,
Of a green galleon.

Ding, ding, ding, ding
Went a bell from the rigging
An English flag was up.

'*Oh No!*' It was the ship
That we sunk in the rip
Of the fiery dawn.

Cannons were manned in the mist
Let loose on that deadly bliss.
'Shoot them down men.'

They did the job in a flash
Jumping aboard with a bash
It was a bloody battle *Ahh!*

Glenn Pooley (9)
Launceston CP School

THE SEA TRIP

Dolphins dive through the sea
To come and meet you and me
You and me love to see
Them deep sea diving through the sea.

His dolphin friends call for him.
As they swam on the surface dimly
As I walked the sand dimly
With my dolphin friend swimming timly.

A very small brass band played
They swam till they reached the full bay
It's the end of the day
The dolphins start to have a play.

Dolphins dive through the sea
To come and meet you and me
You and me love to see
Them deep sea diving through the sea.

Sophie Leese (10)
Launceston CP School

ROLLER-COASTER

Roller-coaster whizzing by,
going up the track real high.

Rushing down to the ground,
making a great thundering sound.

It feels like your face is burning,
the wheels underneath are turning.

Faster than a speeding train,
shaking up your brain.

Children think it's exciting,
and adults think it's frightening.

A crazy cart whooshing past,
this wild thing is so fast.

Candy floss is on the seats,
where the people sit and eat.

Up and down the coaster goes,
then you start to screw up your toes.

A roller-coaster is entertaining,
some people are complaining.

Screaming, shouting at the fair,
twisting, turning, through the air.

Some people wonder who's steering,
and then their heart fills with fear.

Down at the ground,
there's not a single sound.

The wind flies in your face,
it's faster than a Grand Prix race.

Then it starts to stop,
and you feel like you're going to drop.

Melissa Wadman (11)
Launceston CP School

THE SEA TRIP

I was walking across the sand
When something strange happened,
The sea came in over the land
So I started to swim.

Something heavy pulled at my toe,
Then fish swam around me
I looked down as the crabs swam low,
So I went down with them.

There were crabs, sharks, fish and seals.
The crabs pinched and fish swam
Then we went by cod and eels,
I liked the coloured fish.

Then we went past an octopus,
And found somewhere to eat.
Just then we saw a porpoise
It's the first one I'd seen.

I had really enjoyed my day,
But it was time to go
I would have really liked to stay,
But I had to go home.

Avril Wicks (10)
Launceston CP School

THE SEA TRIP

I saw a dolphin in the sea.
As I walked along the beach.
I found a lucky old key
The rocks clashing into the waves.

As I sailed my big yacht
I went back home
As I tied a big knot
I made tea for myself.

I held my pet dog.
I heard a noise outside on the beach
So I put my shoes on
And I wondered, wondered what it was.

Along the beach I heard nothing
I heard a voice.
Help, she's bluffing
Who? And where are you?

I saw a dolphin in the sea
As I walked along the beach.
I found a lucky old key,
The rocks clashing into the waves.

The dolphin hears me scream,
I feel as cold, as cold as ice-cream.
They've come to rescue me.
Can I survive in the deep sea?

I gave them a cuddle
And one gave me a snuggle
Their beaks are like a knife.
I can't believe they saved my life.

I don't want to go home.
The sea is like a big dome.
They are blue like the sea
They are no strangers to me.

I got very wet hair
We need to go up for air
I will feel so alone,
Because I have to go home.

I woke up feeling glad
I never feel very sad.
I went out today
Swimming with the dolphins and to play.

Sarah Harvey (9)
Launceston CP School

THE SEA TRIP

Away we go over seas
Splashing through the muddy waves,
Drifting past the boat so bright.
Hear the stars on a summer's night.

Away we go through the sky
Passing through clouds so bright.
Away we go over Mars
Looking at the beautiful stars.

Hear the water, splish, splash, splish, splash,
Drifting safely on a midsummer night.
Darkness rose into the sky
A happy ending came to die.

Soraya Besley (9)
Launceston CP School

THE SEA TRIP

I ran along the sea shore,
I went to the sea to play,
I came back and saw my spore,
On a hot summer's day.

I swam in the sea,
We climbed to the top,
We played you and me,
It was a big drop.

The sun was shining,
The sea was blue,
I like observing,
The sea view.

The sand was dry,
The sea swayed and swept,
It started to rain I sighed,
The day past and the sun set.

I ran along the sea shore,
I went to the sea to play,
I came back and saw my spore,
On a hot summer's day.

Madeline Horn (9)
Launceston CP School

THE SEA TRIP

Over the blue
We swiftly go
The boat tossing to and fro.

Fish swimming
Under the sea
A chest might lie with a key.

Starfish spread out
Crabs crawl to hide
Sea horses swimming side by side.

The Great White Shark
Lurks all around
The seaweed, and he has found

A sunken ship
Rusty and dark
The boat lies in Neptune's Park.

Live in wonder
Down by the sea
A magical place to be.

Georgina Bradshaw (10)
Launceston CP School

BUBBLES

I am enormous when I float in the air
I move over the tops of the trees
When I see a sharp wave of light from a needle
I feel like it's coming close to me and it might want to eat me
I pop as I vanish in powdery sparkling liquid
I disappear in a puff and nobody can see me.

Laura Hall (7)
Launceston CP School

BUBBLES

Bubbles fly in the sky.
Passing all the trees.
They float past the rivers.
They are brightly coloured.
As pretty as rainbows.
All different sizes.
Big, small, fat and thin.
All as light as a feather.
They shine like gold.
They float high up in the sky.
Like the soft fluffy clouds.
They join together.
Bubbles are great
But when they bump into something,
They pop and are gone.

David Rundle (8)
Launceston CP School

MOORLAND WALKING

At night, a person comes walking, creeping.
In a dark shadow.
As he creeps for twenty-four hours, it is silent.
The night is gloomy.
The path is dark.
He tiptoes, creeps, walks any time of the day.
Morning, afternoon, evening, night.
Even from dawn to dusk.
He leaves his footprints behind.
He climbs up a hill and down.
Jumps up and jumps down.
Left to right, side to side.

Now it is dawn, morning is waking up
But the human is still stepping over rocks,
With a rucksack on his back.
In the hot sun, he rests.
Disappears in the evening to dusk.
Footprints still lying on the land.
There for nearly another hundred centuries.
Still silent.

Emma Cole (10)
Launceston CP School

Bubbles

I am a bubble
I twist and twirl past waterfalls.
I float past trees
I am squashy.
I'm as bright as a rainbow
I shine in the moonlight
I glitter in the sunlight
I stick on the ground.
I sprinkle and twinkle like a star
I feel like a diamond
Then I bounced on the floor
And silently popped on a thorn
I disappeared.
No one could see me
Not even a bubble
Not even a fly.

Poppy Rosen-Jones (7)
Launceston CP School

BUBBLES

Bubbles float in the air silently.
People pop them as they pass by.
When they pop they pop past, very fast.
Sometimes they float slowly.
One pop, two pops, three pops and four pops.
Rainbow colours brighten the sky.
Blue, green, red, gold.
Slow rain comes down on me as they drift by.
Shining as the sun shines.
When they pass by they pass over the trees.
They glow like the sun.
They are as light as a feather.
Darting in and out of the trees.
Colourful as a rainbow.
As delicate as a butterfly.
Popping on the trees as they drift past.
In the gentle breeze.
Bubbles are shining like a watch.
Come to me, pop on my hand.
Come to me and pop.

Gemma Rickard (8)
Launceston CP School

THE MOOR

The wind was whistling in pillars of gloomy darkness
On a murky, deserted plain.
The rain was battering down in torrents
And lacerating rocks.

The windswept grassland.
Of this bare wild place
Was crowded with pounded heather
And marred gorse.

Shadows as dark as a wolf's mouth,
Were scattered all over the moor,
The grey mist came down all round,
I was lost in the dead of the night.

I stumbled on through thick and thin
While the storm raged on
I was thankful to see a twinkling village
To shelter me from the tempest.

Tristan Tremain (11)
Launceston CP School

BUBBLES

A tiny bubble comes out from nowhere.
Then bigger, bigger and bigger.
It floats the trees.
It feels great as it floats.
It is going to fly everywhere.
England, Mexico, Denmark, Wales.
Everywhere until *Bang!*
Then lots of other bubbles come
They drift through the sky.
I watch them *Pop!*
Lots of big, small round footballs come
To invade.
The small ones *pop.*
The big ones float over the hills and far away.
Shiny lovely bubbles come to play.

Caillin Astles (8)
Launceston CP School

THE MOOR

Upon the bracken littered moor,
The wind blows wild,
Ripping through the lone gorse.

Sheep munch on the moors grassy undergrowth,
They move absorbing the wind,
As the driving rain pounds them,
As they find shelter in the lees of gorse.

And here and there lone houses lie,
Cut off from the rest of the world,
A thick blanket of smoke pours out of the chimneys
From the glowing fires within their walls.

The wind slashes against the rocky faces of tors,
As they stand tall fighting the elements.
Slowly weathering away.

Great chimney stacks of an industry long gone,
Rise from the bracken like fingers.
Slowly crumbling with the passing of time.
Being bombarded by wind.

Great quarries long left to flood,
And swamped with reeds,
Feel the power of the wind driven rain,
As they lie helpless and deserted.
On the moors open planes.

Hawthorn is played with like a cat with a mouse.
By the savage wind,
As it sweeps low over the moor,
Wreaking havoc.

On into the night the storm rages,
But by morning it had gone,
To terrify somewhere else.

Jeremy Cole (11)
Launceston CP School

BUBBLE

I float around the flowers.
I dangle around.
I shine from top to bottom.
Maybe I am light but I still go up.
I dive down to the ground.
I am slim. I find people popping me
With a pin.
I go quick.
I wiggle through the trees.
People say I am little.
I go up and up.
I see other bubbles.
We join in tow.
I go to the floor.
I *pop.*

Here I come again,
I go up to see the sunshine,
As golden as sand.
I get too hot then I go down
And crash in the flowers.

Rachel Ponsford (8)
Launceston CP School

BUBBLES

I am floating, floating like a
Star in the sky.
I float very high.
I am as round as a ball.
I float through trees.
I am as bright as the moon.
I am as bouncy as a ball.
I bounce very tall.
I am as transparent as glass.
I twirl above the grass.
I am as shiny as gold.
I twinkle like a star
I am fast just like a racing car.

Elliot Michael Cole (7)
Launceston CP School

I AM THE BUBBLE

I can drift slow and silent.
Over trees and waterfalls.
I float into the sunset
And over the hills
I look like a shiny rainbow
I do like to float gently in the breeze
Bubbles joining together
Just like a family
Some can go slower
I drift over the lake
I suddenly float down, down
Then I pop.

Amy Maunder (7)
Launceston CP School

BUBBLES

I am a bubble floating through the jungle.
I turn round and round like a roundabout,
I am transparent.
I can also bounce onto the leaves and make the water drip off them
And onto the cool steamy ground.
When I am floating I change shape so quickly that nobody notices
Sometimes when I am floating I bump into other bubbles and we all
join together like snow.
When we are together we sparkle like a star.
When I am in the sky I look and feel like a cloud.
Sometimes I hit a lump and pop into a speck of dust.
Sometimes I float down and pop suddenly on the ground.

Merryn Parnell (7)
Launceston CP School

IF I WERE A BUBBLE

If I were to be a bubble,
I'd be as tiny as an ant.
I would be as golden as the sunrise
Floating all around.
The colours would be beautiful!
I wish I could be a bubble.
High up in the sky.
Looking down at all the plants
Fluffy clouds high above me
But when I pop
I would fall like tiny raindrops.

Kimberley Bond Webber (8)
Launceston CP School

BUBBLES SWIM IN THE AIR

I like to fly anywhere with a golden tint
I like to pop up in the sky and fly over land.
I fly fast through the blue sky in the day, black sky at night.
Float and stick to anything.
My shell is as cold as the Arctic.
I glitter in the sky as bright as a star.
I slide into boulders like volcano lava.
I dash over schools and cities.
I see all artefacts, sky scrapers and statues.
I glide into house windows.
Bubbles swim, bubbles float.
I fly through the air like a supersonic jet.
Suddenly I pop on a dustbin lid.
I float into the black bubble heaven.

Kieran Hancock (7)
Launceston CP School

THE BUBBLE

I float across a meadow.
I'm purple, green and red.
Cows look in fright.
I float to a waterfall.
Like an aeroplane to land.
Down I float by the waterfall.
I land on the water.
I float miles and miles.
I float over the hills and far away.

Rupert Freestone (8)
Launceston CP School

THE WIND

It comes out in the dead of the night.
As it thumps,
It bites.
The gale-force wind,
batters the door,
And spreads litter,
About the floor.
As I hear it in my bed,
A world is spinning in my head,
Whirling around,
The torn branches fall down,
Making no headway
To the middle of the town.
As the wind shatters a gate,
Off the roof comes some slate,
As my cat jumped on my head,
A dream of dreams is inside my head.

Michael Diebner (11)
Launceston CP School

IF I WAS A BUBBLE

If I was a bubble
I would float over
Flowers and trees.
I would float as high as the wind that blows
I would drift over cornfields.
I would hover over people
I float down and down and down.
I would float up and up and up,
Then I would *pop.*

Zoe Sefton (7)
Launceston CP School

BUBBLES

I float like a balloon and fly like a bird.
I fly through the trees gently.
People pop me then blow me up again.
People see me floating over a waterfall.
I sparkle like a diamond.
I shine like the moon.
I twist like a whirlwind.
I fly as fast as an eagle.
I balance like a ballerina.
I'm as light as a feather.
When I rest I am,
        Gone!

Amy Louise Rogers (7)
Launceston CP School

BUBBLE

I am a bubble
So gold and pretty
Small and round
As light as a feather
I float over the hills
And I glide like a bird
Springing up and down
As bouncy as a pogo stick
I am as shiny as the sun
as silly as a worm
I twinkle like the stars.

Peter Hatch (8)
Launceston CP School

THE SEA STORM

The dark, raging, sea was twisting with phenomenal turbulence
                                                    like a tornado,
Ships were struggling and trying to avoid the powerful swirling winds.
Waves like black blankets slapping against the windbeaten cliffs and
                                                    shingly shore.
Thoughts of the worst puzzling the minds of people watching in horror.
I looked out of my window with anxious eyes, and turned back in
Disgust as I had seen the storm and its angry mind doing it's worst,
And crews that were totally innocent,
Being plunged into the sea as the mighty sea storm struck again.
I heard the violent hiss of the sea spray,
As it spat viciously against the coarse rocks.
And the cries of unfortunate fishermen caught in the storm
As they descended beneath the icy sea.

Georgina Freestone (10)
Launceston CP School

BUBBLES

I am a bubble.

If I was a bubble
I would float about.
In and out of the trees.
I would float about in
Homes, up and down the stairs.
When outside I would float
About up to the sun, and then I pop.

Samuel Jenkins (8)
Launceston CP School

LAMBORGHINI

Speeding like a thunderbolt,
Metallic doors shut tightly,
Turning onto the motorway,
Cool music from open windows.

Switching turbo to twin turbo,
Burning rubber off the tyres,
Changing into fifth gear trying
To break the speed limit,
Smelly smoke and smog filling the air with fumes.

The yellow rectangular beast prowls the road like a
tiger,
Stylish wheels spinning round,
Smooth leather seats, shining glass,
Roaring revs, engine hot.

Chris Jeffery (11)
Launceston CP School

BUBBLES

I'm flying over tops of trees.
I'm flying up in the sky.
I pop on people's heads.
Sometimes I like to stick to other bubbles.
Sometimes I pop and turn into a puff of smoke.
I'm like a bean floating in the sky.
I'm wobbling like a jellyfish floating up high.
Quick! Quick! I'm going to pop into a puff of smoke.
I see everything up high like the shop and the swimming pool.

Claire Wicks (7)
Launceston CP School

GLOOMY NIGHT

In the night
A fox was scavenging
In the dustbin
For food.
Stars were shining
On his beautiful glistening coat
As he looked up at me
Frightened and scared.
Moonbeams shone on houses
Glistening in the night
Mist took over the land
Everywhere it was dark
And gloomy
When he ran off into
The distance.

James Penfold (10)
Launceston CP School

WHEN I SAW A BUBBLE

When I saw a bubble it was as gold
As the sun.
When I saw a bubble it was
As wet as water.
When I saw a bubble
It popped into a river.
When I saw a bubble it was as colourful as a rainbow.
When I saw a bubble it was as soft as a cloud.
When I have popped it into a puddle,
I make another bubble.

Daniel Vidler (7)
Launceston CP School

THE WOOD

A dark, gloomy wood,
stands high on the hill,
in the middle of nowhere,
hiding dark secrets.

A meandering murky river,
snakes through thorny branches,
stagnant water flowing,
no life forms swim in it.

A never-ending,
leaf covered path,
twists and turns,
and leads you nowhere.

Moonlit eyes,
light up the darkness,
blinking on and off,
darting left and right.

Unknown creatures,
stalk the night,
searching for prey,
waiting to pounce.

The howling wind,
claws at the leaves,
screaming and shouting,
breaking the silence of the night.

A dark, gloomy wood,
stands high on the hill,
in the middle of nowhere,
Hiding dark secrets.

Joe Pooley (11)
Launceston CP School

THE TORNADO

The twisting tornado towers the Earth.
It was once a breeze but from its birth
It travelled over oceans wide.
Twisting and turning from side to side.

The twisting tornado gathering up trees,
Gliding over rivers and world-wide seas,
Sweeping fish from the ocean bed,
Not many survive, so it's said.

The force began to grow inside,
As people ran away to hide.
Lives were going to be turned around.
As the force of the storm struck the ground.

The wind died down and the storm disappeared,
It had left a mess as the people had feared,
Lives were destroyed and ripped apart,
As families were left with a hole in the heart.

From the destruction a new life was born,
The buildings and people were ripped and torn.
The worst was now over but there was still fear,
Another tornado could be ever so near.

Katie Probert (10)
Launceston CP School

GHOSTS AND GHOULS

The clock struck twelve,
The house came to life,
All the ghosts and ghouls came out at midnight.

Blood-curdling screams,
Hair-raising groans,
All the blood in my body ran cold to my bones.

My heart pounding like thunder,
And echoing in my head,
Like a flash of lightning I leapt out of bed.

Where could I run to?
Where could I hide?

How long will this night go on for?
And will I survive?

Out of nowhere came a beam of daylight,
All the ghosts and ghouls got a terrible fright.

With a sudden flash,
All the ghosts and ghouls were gone,
I screamed for my mum,
And turned the light on.

Chauntelle Besley (11)
Launceston CP School

I Can Hear!

I can hear the cold winds blow
As I grow to know
The chiming clock bells.

I bend my head back to
catch the wind in my
face as my mother packs my
favourite case.

It's hard to swallow
because the wind is
pounding in my face
and it's hard to read
my favourite book 'Ace'.

The wind blows and blows
and blows . . .
        Blows

Chloe Rogers (9)
Mylor Bridge School

The Seagull

The sneak
He's the sneaky one
Thief of the beach
Muncher of time
The sneak
The sneaky one
That pecks and wrecks
Squeaks and shrieks
He's the mean one
The sneak.

Joseph Walker (9)
Nancledra School

A SPACE TRAVELLER

Way up here in the dark of night
See those stars to he left to the right,
Up and down
All around
It truly is an amazing sight,
See the sun
See the moon
See the plants
Zoom and Zoom
And then the moon
It blinds me.
Oh so bright.
The Earth swirly and blue
It is great from this view.
The Milky Way
A big white gleaming gate.
I wish I could come here all the time,
It feels like a wonderful dream.
I love this dream,
It is so peaceful,
When I get home I can look up and say
What a wonderful place is space.

Zac John Birchley (10)
Nancledra School

THE PENGUIN

She waddles out of
the icy sea
So ignorant and
greedy she
can be.
Shivering islands of
frost glimmer free.
Silky black,
light, white
feathers bundled
up tightly together,
Feeling the breath of the
freezing cold
weather.

Tomas Griffin (9)
Nancledra School

THE PARROT

He glides through trees
like a streaming
rainbow.
Colourful wings softly
they flow.
Proud of himself his
eyes glow.
He hides in trees like
autumn leaves.
His tail is bright and his
feet are light
As he perches in the
trees.

Elizabeth Birchley (10)
Nancledra School

LONELY MAN

I'm a lonely man up in space
With nothing to do but look at the Earth's face.
I look at Saturn with all its rings,
And wonder what made those beautiful
things,
I look at Venus with its pink outer crust,
I look at the clouds made of solar dust,
I see the sun starting a day,
I see the moon so far away,
I look at Pluto so small and green,
It looks very much like a large butter bean,
I'm a lonely man up in space,
With nothing to do but look at the Earth's face.

Timmy Thompson (11)
Nancledra School

DARK, DARK SPACE

A rocket in dark, dark space
Finding new things for the human race
When I look up into that place
There is no trace
That a rocket has been in space

We have the technology to send a
man to the moon when he is seventy years old
But we still can't cure the common cold.

Harrison Evans (10)
Nancledra School

A DIAMOND

Space is like a lung eternally expanding for all time,
It began many times smaller than a human and began
to grow and grow.
As a tiny seed grows into a mighty tree and spreads out all its leaves,
the universe began to grow
In half a second it grew to twice the size of the sun!
We are the fruits of this 'Mighty Tree' for in us are the tree's destiny.
What else existed outside the universe when it was in its seed like form?
Nothing, and maybe not even time.
Time, as if some sand timer, the sand stuck in its position
then a grain slipped and time began.
So in such a vast and great universe run by things no one could imagine,
why on earth would you need something as strange as life?
You may want to think of us as colours to a picture,
for without colours it has no life.
Or maybe we are the flickering light found in a diamond gem.

Ross Becalick (11)
Nancledra School

ONE BIG FAMILY

Look at those stars
They smile and shine down on you.
They are like balls of gas

The moon is their mother
She guides them
Gives the signal to come out.

The sun is their guard
As they sleep in the clouds.

Is space endless darkness?

Rosie Chapman (11)
Nancledra School

JUPITER

What is Jupiter?
A jolly face,
A child's ball bouncing,
A raindrop on a rainbow,
A sweet in a shop,
An eye glancing at you,
A ball, a nut, a merry-go-round,
I think Jupiter is a bird flying,
Green, blue, pink and yellow,
The size of the palm of my hand,
As hot as a spark from a fire,
Jupiter moves with the dreams and songs of space.

Emma Nankervis (9)
Nancledra School

THE OWL

Watching his prey with one eye,
Thinking to himself
'You're going to die.'
Hovering about in the sky,
Swooping to the ground,
Like a glider,
Not a sound.
Then . . .
Munch!
Crunch!
The animal he had found
Had gone.

Matthew King (9)
Nancledra School

THE SUN

The sun is a creature burning bright,
Way brighter than Mr Moon, who lights up the night.
The sun is a star that lights up the Earth,
The Earth must be blessing the day of it's birth.
The sun is a hothouse at tons of degrees,
On the sun there is *never* a very slight breeze.
Like thousands of volcanoes it should be out of your sight,
Or you'll be banging into trees for the rest of your sad life.
The sun's generation is very bad-tempered
He would like to tessellate with others to become the biggest star,
As king of the solar system he should be content.
Mercury, Venus, our Earth, Mars,
Jupiter, Saturn, Uranus, Neptune and poor old Pluto
Must be getting teased every second by Mr Sun,
For not being half as bright or strong,
But one day . . .
There will be none of them.

Orlando Bird (8)
Nancledra School

STARS

Up there in the dead of night
Balls of gas burning bright
Lighting up the universe
One day they might just burst
If they do
They'll kill the humans
And the Earth
The sun will no longer light up our sky
The universe will no longer be
An amazing sight.

Lawrence Kennedy (11)
Nancledra School

FORWARD INTO DARKNESS

As the countdown comes to end
I wonder if this is my fate to be,
To find new life
And make peace,
Then leave again
To explore.
Looking out of my window
I see a bright light.
From time to time
A star flies by,
To my surprise.
Being a space traveller
That's the life for me.
Being a free man,
To do whatever I like.
Maybe not everyone's cup of tea.
But sadly,
My journey has to come to an end.

Christopher Olds (11)
Nancledra School

QUESTIONS

What is that bright light zooming through the sky?
A shooting star?
A streaming comet?
No, a jumbo jet.

What's that bright white light way up in the sky?
The sun white hot?
Or perhaps the moon?
No, a white, hot air balloon.

What's that huge black dip in the depths of outer space?
The final gate?
Or my imagination?
Nobody could ever answer that question.

Where do the stars go when it's daylight bright?
To another world?
Or just disappear?
We know they're there, we just can't find them.

Guthrie Musser (10)
Nancledra School

SPACE

S pace a giant ocean waiting to be discovered.
P lanets, moons and stars sprinkled over
   the night sky like hundreds and
   thousands on top of a cake.
A steroids and comets shoot through space like they're
   at the head of a race.
C onquering space is no easy mission for space goes on
   and on and on for all eternity.
E scaping the vast clutches of space is
   impossible.

Alf Brockett (11)
Nancledra School

THE PAPER'S POINT OF VIEW

I hate being paper I really do,
People cut me and stick me down with glue.
They leave me on their beds,
And throw me at teachers heads!
I hate being paper I really do.
People score on me.
Children waste me by throwing me
away for no reason.
They print ink on me that's cold and wet
Adults read stories of me like Macbeth!
The millennium's coming Oh no! What a
threat,
More children to waste me,
More children to scrunch and scribble
on me.
I really hate being paper I really do,
Please, please don't waste me.

Jacqueline Luckham (10)
St Ives Junior School, Cornwall

SEASIDE

The clouds are fluffy and white and
They are like ice cream.
The sea is soft and smooth and blue.
The sand is like gold from the sun.

Emily Rowe (9)
St Ives Junior School, Cornwall

SCHOOL DINNERS

The chips taste of cardboard,
The peas are bullet hard,
The mash is cold,
The sausages are soggy,
The soup tastes like chalk,
The cream is out of date,
I suppose the disco food is OK,
But school dinners are not,
The yoghurt, you'll have to guess the flavour,
Loads of dinners are wasted
Scrape scrape go the plates,
Ice-creams are rock solid,
They taste of muck,
I only wish school dinners were more nice.

James McGovern (10)
St Ives Junior School, Cornwall

SEASIDE

The seaside is really rather grand,
The seagulls swooping and squawking,
Fluffy clouds of ice-cream,
The sun is as gold as the sand.

Daniel Rouncefield (9)
St Ives Junior School, Cornwall

THERE'S A GHOST IN MY HOUSE

There's a ghost in my house.
Swooping my stairs.
Growling and howling.
Round he who dares.
Staring and glaring.
With his spooky red eyes.
Coming closer and closer,
I'm dying with fright
Boo!
There's a ghost in my room,
Please take it away.

Catherine Powell (11)
St Ives Junior School, Cornwall

SEASIDE

The seaside is lovely and warm,
Even the ice-cream looks like big fluffy clouds,
The blue sea is smooth and soft,
The sand is like the sun shining on the pure gold,
The gull's swooping down and stealing food,
But the sea is like a roaring lion.

Hannah Rose Rimmer (9)
St Ives Junior School, Cornwall

MILLENNIUM

Millennium,
Millennium,
Bells are ringing
It's a new beginning.

Millennium,
Millennium
Let's start singing
And celebrating.

Millennium,
Millennium,
Parties and projects,
People will be praying
It's a new century
So start singing

Millennium,
Millennium,
Parties for you and
Parties for me.

Robbie Williams
Will be singing
Millennium.

In the year 2000AD

New life
New shops
New Century

Emily Kessell (10)
St Merryn School, Padstow

MILLENNIUM

Now the millennium
Is almost here,
Then we have to wait
Another thousand years.

Soon will come
The 21st Century,
Everyone can't wait
Including me.

I don't believe
In the Millennium Bug,
Because how could that thing
Turn off a plug?

For me I'll see it
Once in my life,
And I know one thing
No one will see it twice.

I won't be here
To see it next time,
Because if I did
I'll be 909.

I also like the song
That Robbie Williams sang.
I think he'll have a concert
With fireworks that go bang.

I don't think I will make it
To the Millennium Dome,
I just think that I will have
A party of my own.

The millennium is heard
Around the Earth,
Because it is the world's
Most popular birth.

Bryn Dolman (10)
St Merryn School, Padstow

MILLENNIUM

New beginning.
New century.

Robbie Williams new songs,
Even Steps maybe,
but there's only got to be one song
because there's the Millennium Dome.

New lives,
New shops,
New cars,
and even new money.

Ships upon the seas,
Plenty of fish for everybody,
Over the lands.

People getting wed,
Church bells ringing.
Even happiness is going round.

Diseases going round,
lots of people getting it,
Many people are still homeless,
even with no place to go or eat.

Hollie Cogdale (10)
St Merryn School, Padstow

THE MILLENNIUM

The first thing that I think about,
Has got to be the Dome.
You would have to be mad,
To keep yourself at home.

If your computer catches the Millennium Bug,
Then your work could be at risk,
So make a note and be prepared,
Save all your work on a disk.

Should we say two thousand,
Or, will twenty hundred be the norm.
I wish someone would tell us,
Because I'm feeling very torn.

What will the millennium hold,
I wish that I could see.
And will we still live above the ground,
Or in a dome at the bottom of the sea.

No one knows where we will be,
A century from here,
We may evolve and grow two heads,
Or on our chin a triple ear.

If I had a crystal ball,
A fortune I would make.
I could see just what the future holds
And what would be my fate.

On the eve of the millennium,
For my friends I'd throw a party.
I would dress up as a pirate,
And say ahoy me hearty.

No matter what we do or say,
We know one thing for sure,
At the end of 1999,
The new millennium, knocks upon the door.

Benjamin Lee Milby (11)
St Merryn School, Padstow

THE MILLENNIUM

The New Century - of new things
Future vehicles - made into new cars
Lots of parties - with Robbie Williams
New life - New shops
New beginnings - very rare
Church bells ringing - all over the place
2000 *very near*
The Millennium Bug - like a disease
Two weeks on the Moon?
Cures for cancer - aids -asthma?
Shoes that float - on water - in the air
Divers that can go - to the bottom of the sea
Will cars fly - instead of going on wheels?
Will there be a cure - for blind to see again?
Will there be a cure - for deaf to hear again?
Police cars - that can go up to 2000 miles per hour
or perhaps - *no crime at all.*
I wish I could be here for the next millennium.

Chris Thomas (10)
St Merryn School, Padstow

MILLENNIUM

Say goodbye to 1999
Let's hope for more sunshine.

The year 2000 is dawning
let everybody stop warring.

Everybody will be celebrating
the era of a new millennium.

Eden dome
Will nearly be complete
With all types of plants
For us to see.

Starvation and poverty, a thing of the past
food and water for the great mass.

New classrooms
and gym for the school
Although it means
Saying goodbye to the pool.

Celebrating and parties to welcome the New Year
laughing and clapping, people in good cheer.

Miners and farmers
back to work
This is not a time to lie down and
shirk.

Beef on the bone
back on the shelf
We should have been
able to please ourself.

Karl Hughes (10)
St Merryn School, Padstow

MILLENNIUM

The music is blaring
and everyone is wearing
their favourite party clothes.

Everyone is drunk
when a man gets a thump.
Everyone will have a hangover
when I'm eating my clover.
There are street parties all over town
when the Queen is watching her crown.

The computers are going
dumb, but they will die
and why?

Everyone is buying
but no one is crying.
Go and buy a new car
and travel a far.
Buy a boat, but watch
it might not float.
Some cunning people could
win that money.

I was reading a book and
my mum hired a cook.

Let's start a fire and
go and hear the school choir.

Go to the Dome and watch the play
on that very special day.

Clark Mills (9)
St Merryn School, Padstow

MILLENNIUM

The year 2000
will soon be here
everyone will be happy
into the New Year.

Goodbye to the nineties
and wishing you all here
then we will go out and
have a few beers.

There will be parties at school
and parties at home
if I'm very lucky
I will see the Millennium Dome.

The dome is big and fat
and will hold lots of people just like that
there will be rides for children
and plenty to do oh my goodness
what shall we do?

On this first day
let's hope and pray
people are nicer
in every way
no more fighting
and no more wars
because it's a new start
that we all long for

It would be nice
to have the peace
of friendships all around
instead of people fighting
all of the time.

Michelle Millard (11)
St Merryn School, Padstow

THE MILLENNIUM

The millennium is very rare
There's going to be new lives to share.
The church bells will be ringing
and we will all be singing
because there is a new beginning.

This will be a once in a lifetime's joy.
For every girl and every boy.
People will rush to leave their home
To see the opening of the Millennium Dome.

In Cornwall there will be a new Garden of Eden
With shrubs and flowers for insects feeding.

I hope the world will be a better place to live
That everyone doesn't just take, but give
And people are nicer to one another
Especially my brother!

Future vehicles and new cars.
Perhaps we will all go up to Mars?
I hope for all diseases there will be a cure.
So deaths and illness will be fewer.

Schools will be better places to learn
And less of the rainforest to burn.

We hope that all starvation will cease
And African nations live in peace.
We hope for peace and happiness forever
And live in harmony together.

I hope the rare species will continue to survive
As long as people live and let live
I hope that my poem all comes true
That the world will be a better place for me and you.

Thea Tomkins (9)
St Merryn School, Padstow

MILLENNIUM

The Century has come to an end
1900 to 2000.
The computer may crash,
oh what a bash.

Songs have been sung,
songs have been written.
New cars are coming,
old cars are going.
New buildings have grown,
new projects have been given.
The great big Millennium Dome,
one of 2000 big investments.

Count down in December,
from the 1st to the 31st.
Party dress to remember,
invitation to be sent.
Lots of preparation,
money to be spent.

Hope everyone makes the party
Fancy dress or plain.
Lots of drink and snacks.
The toast of the Century
to be made.
Lots of laughter
brings hope and joy.

Your place or mine
let's all celebrate.
Make merry the new millennium
2000 has come
Say goodbye to 1999.

Kerry Hughes (11)
St Merryn School, Padstow

MILLENNIUM

It's the millennium next year,
a new life,
a new year,
It's the millennium next year
It will be the year,
2000
2000.

It will be the year 2000,
next year,
next year.
It will be the year 2000,
It is very rare,
very rare,
very rare.

It is very rare indeed it is,
There may be a new disease,
disease,
disease.

There may be a new disease,
It will be a new century,
new century
new century.

It will be a new century.
There may be new computers,
computers,
computers.

There may be new computers and a change,
a change,
a change.
There may be a new change.

Holly Stephens (11)
St Merryn School, Padstow

MILLENNIUM

Robbie Williams and parties
New vehicles, new cars
computers and bugs
New shops, new schools,
new life, new beginning,
new century lots of fun.
Corks popping balloons flying,
fireworks flashing.
New looks, new thoughts
new cushions, new inventions.
Out with the nineteen nineties
In with the year two thousand.
A big fat Dome
A big new life
The millennium is very near
With lots of noise.
Church bells ringing,
Songs being sung
Songs have been written.
Lots of laughter, games being played.
People celebrate with lots of drink
and lots of food.
Flying vehicles and lots of new toys,
lots of new ships.
The millennium is very near.
I won't be here for the next one
So make do with what you've got
Hope everyone makes the party
Fancy dress or plain
Lots of food and drink.
The toast of a century to be made.

Claire Colwill (11)
St Merryn School, Padstow

PEOPLE ARE PREPARING NOW

All the excitement, all the parties,
all the fireworks going bang,
all the people saying 'Wow!'
People are preparing now.

Going on holiday, meeting the Queen,
got a long way to go.
All the people practising how to bow,
People are preparing now.

All the bad things, all the troubles.
The millennium, the Dome.
Just how are we going to manage, just how?
People are preparing now.

All the food, all the water,
What if we run out?
All the people having a row,
People are preparing now.

All the good things, all the bad
What if it goes through to harvest?
What if there's no fuel for the plough?
People are preparing now.

The year 2000 is coming soon,
So I suggest you get ready,
Get some milk from the cow, 'cause maybe . . .
People are preparing now!

Millennium projects are very rare,
there's no need to get a scare.
No diseases or anything like that,
no reason to go ugh, but . . .
People are preparing now.

Rosie Smith (9)
St Merryn School, Padstow

CELEBRATION 2000

It's ten seconds till midnight
This day gave me such a fright
Because this is a new century
Five seconds till midnight
Last year has gone
This year will be much more fun
One second till midnight
Bang
It's the New Year - 2000
The crowd cheered
There were loads of people with beer.

Benjy Tremayne (10)
Trannack CP School

THE YEAR 2000

Balloons and parties everywhere,
The smell of happiness in the air.
Party food and lots of fun,
1999 is on the run.
You'll be happy all the day,
The year 2000's here to stay.

Fay Nicholls (9)
Trannack CP School

CELEBRATION 2000

The millennium is
coming fast and
furious
And all the people are
very curious.
The fun has just begun
And everybody is over
the sun.
The laughter and
singing
All the bells will be
ringing.
Dancing and whirling
And everybody
swirling.
I think the millennium
is done
and now we're in the
year 2001.

Sarah Brilot (10)
Trannack CP School

CELEBRATION 2000

I have just shaken hands
with everyone in sight
it is tonight,
counting from ten down to
one
and I
am having lots of fun.

Vicki Girling (11)
Trannack CP School

CELEBRATION 2000

10 seconds till midnight
10, 9, 8, 7, 6, millennium is in sight
5, 4, 3, the suspense is growing
What will people be doing?
2, 1, the millennium has begun.
The last year has been fun
But this year is going to be brill
it's also going to be a thrill
Back to celebrating until next year
The new millennium is well and truly here.

Sally Beach (11)
Trannack CP School

YEAR 2000

The clang of glasses in the air
And bubbles on the floor.
A party popper going off 12 o'clock is
nearly there.
The computers are crashing
Then it's here a great big cheer
For the New Year and then it was all over.

Oliver Bywaters (11)
Trannack CP School

CELEBRATIONS 2000

If you want a celebration this
is where you should be
if you want a celebration listen
to me,
This Is The Next Millennium!

Harry Newman (9)
Trannack CP School

PETS

At last my dog Max caught the ball.
Ginger my cat sleeps on the wall.
Jabber the parrot always talks.
Nibbles the hamster chews wine corks.

Why did my tortoise run so fast?
Our worms had a race. Mine came last.
I've about fifty fishes
But I have many wishes.

Why can't my pony jump a five foot fence?
He thought it was quite immense.
Lucy my goat always butts.
Ouch! Now I have many cuts.

My rabbit loves his lettuce.
He never ever lets us
Play with the duck
But the problem is he gives me good luck.

People think lots of pets are a handful
But I like my pet life to be full.

Celine Phillips (11)
Treliske School

THE TIGER

The tiger lurks
Amongst the grass
Waiting for its prey
At last
A deer walks past
Unaware
The danger that is lurking there.

The tiger pounces
Upon the deer
Cutting short
Its dread and fear
It grabs it
With its shark like jaws
Clinging with its ruthless claws.

Hunger satisfied
The tiger licks
Its bloody lips
And slinks into the night
Leaving the deer
Who lost its fight
For life.

Emma Pearson (11)
Treliske School

SNAKES

Snakes are scaly
Slippery and sleek
They slither up to you
And make you say, 'eek!'

They slide through the grass
Waiting for a fly to come past.
They stick out their tongue
And swallow it fast.

James Hollins (10)
Treliske School

A DAY AT SEA

Setting off towards the ocean
Towards the blue and green
The mysterious and the deep blue sea
With peculiar creatures I've never seen.

We leave the shore behind us
And now we're on our own
The gulls are crying overhead
As we bob up and down on the foam.

We see the land and it's tall trees
It's shells and sands on the shore
We then, spot a quiet cove
For us to go and moor.

We throw out the anchor
And jump into the tender
We fasten up the rowlocks
And push off from the fender.

We eat our supper on the beach
Quickly now it's twilight
We just have time to gather our things
And head back to the boat before night.

Kitty Jenkin (10)
Treliske School

CATS

Cats in the dark,
With their glistening eyes.
They move like darts,
When they pounce on flies.

They sit with you,
And watch TV.
They make holes in your clothes,
And make bread on your knee.

Cats love fishing
In a garden pond.
They hook the fish,
Like agent James Bond!

They creep in the night
Into your bed,
Then when you wake up,
They're asleep on your head!

Cats can climb trees,
Mine fall off them!
When they're left alone
They can cause mayhem.

Cats are frequent bird watchers,
It's one of their favourite games.
They eat them, then vomit them up,
Including all the brains!

William Penrose (11)
Treliske School

CLOTHES

Humans wear them all the time,
Even when they're sleeping,
They wear them in the park,
And they wear them when they're eating.

Some are silk and some are cotton,
Some have stripes and some have spots on,
Children wear clothes to school,
Because it is the school rule.

Skirts and shirts are for girls,
They wear them with their shiny pearls
Trousers and shorts are for boys,
They wear them playing with their toys.

So all in all everyone knows,
We couldn't live without our clothes.

Laura Wing (11)
Treliske School

MY DOG

My dog's name is Ralphie
He's a fierce little chap.
He runs around yelling up and down the stairs;
Knocking over tables and knocking over chairs.
He loves to chew letters when they come through the box.
I've even seen him eyeing one of my smelly old socks.
There's not much more to say.
He's perfect in every way.
Even though he has some faults,
He's mine and he's here to stay.

Christian Hicks (11)
Treliske School

MY FIRST LESSON

I'm quite a naughty boy
And I'm really very small,
My sister is twice as tall as me,
'Help me with my tea!' my mum calls.

I didn't even hear her,
And my sister didn't notice,
'Help me with my tea!' mum calls again,
'Or your sister will give you a kiss!'

I was terrified by the thought,
And a shiver went down my spine,
Nearer and nearer the lips came,
'Wait mum,' I cried, 'I'm coming to dine!'

Mum thought I went too far,
It was time for her to get back,
It was horrible, scary, terrible, mad.
She dyed my hair black!

My mum had got revenge,
And she forced me to paint her toes,
How was I going to get back at her,
Anyway, who knows?

Rico Wong (10)
Treliske School

FOOTBALL

I've got a big game it's coming up tomorrow,
I hope we don't lose and end up in sorrow.
We'll probably win and take the gold,
Because staff and parents are really old!
Then they'll be battering each other's eyelids,
Because they got beaten by a bunch of kids.

We'll all score a goal each,
And Tom will make a brilliant speech.
That's how I think the match will go.
We'll wait and see,
I think I know!

Nicholas Westgarth (11)
Treliske School

THE WITCH

Cackles fill the air,
The wind blows back her hair.
She flies past on her broomstick,
And all the children stare.

Her nose is long and hooked,
With fingers bent and crooked.
To see her is so rare,
So all the children stare.

Cold and dirty her legs hang down,
She turns and gives an angry frown,
Her skirt is patched, and has a tear,
And all the children stare.

Behind the witch there clings her cat,
A ferocious terrible cat that spat.
It's eyes give out a piercing glare,
And all the children stare.

With a sparkle and a flash of light,
The broomstick leaps to a great height.
Then disappears into the night,
And all the children stare.

Amy Morse (10)
Treliske School

TIGERS

The tiger's stripes are nice and bright
In the forest day and night
Searching and roaming for their prey
The victim, of course, has no say!

The prey young, innocent, yet healthy and good
I want to save him, if only I could,
Evil, hungry, vicious and bad,
The tiger waits to make his prey sad.

The tiger creeps up licking his lips,
Waiting to chew on a victim's hips.
The prisoner is scared and frightened,
the woods around him tighten.

The tiger was ready to eat
From the victim's head to his feet.

The victim is dead,
The tiger is fed.

Ben Radford   (10)
Treliske School

WHAT HAPPENS IN THE CLASSROOM AT NIGHT?

What happens in the classroom,
When all the lights are off,
I have always wondered.
What happens in the classroom every night.

All the tables play push and shove.
The chairs think it's a gym.
The radio turns on full volume.
The clock juggles batteries.

The filing cabinet stands on one corner,
Things on posters come to life.
Lockers open and shut their doors,
Pins come out and work falls down.

At the cleaner's footsteps,
Everything picks itself up.
All is back to normal,
No one notices a thing.

Sarah King (10)
Treliske School

My Dog

Floppy ears,
Large nose,
Long tail,
In a pose.

Hair like my dad,
Very curly and mad.
She has lots of bounce,
Especially when chasing a mouse.

Brown eyes,
Eats dad's ties.
When you're eating meat,
She begs at your feet.

She's as gentle as a dove,
And gets lots of love.
Even when she's tired,
She is always admired.

Milly Freeman (11)
Treliske School

Seasons

Spring brings new things.
Animals are born.
Flowers open,
Birds sing.
Spring is full of wonderful things.

I like Spring!

Summer sun is so hot.
Eclipse this year.
Busy beaches,
Full hotels,
I think I'll go diving off the pier.

I like Summer!

Autumn is a cold time of year.
Leaves fall from trees.
Red leaves,
Green leaves,
It's that time of year.

I like Autumn!

Winter brings wonderful things.
The coldest time of year.
Christmas and snow,
Courage and cheer,
Winter's the best time of year.

I like Winter!

Daisy op de Weegh (10)
Treliske School

WINTER

Winter is a cold old season,
everything is cold and frozen.
Snow comes down and covers the earth,
in a thin and silky coat.

Everyone goes outside to play,
throwing snowballs and building snowmen.
Skating outside on the lake,
and skiing down the hill

But when the snow melts away
they're back to playing football.
Going to the park,
and going swimming too.

Aaron Edgcumbe (11)
Treliske School

PORTH JOKE

It's a long walk,
Along a path,
A sharp-stoned beach,
At the start.

Further on,
The sand is soft,
The sea a shimmering blue,
The rocks are smooth and black,
The cliff's high and green,
There's a wonderful path amongst the hills,
And a campsite right next to the stream.

Mawgan Taylor (10)
Treliske School

SKATING ON MY DECK

I like to go skating
It is so great.
I do kickflips as I watch my mate.

Doing grinds along a rail
Screeching turns leave a trail.

I push away fast.
Up the half pipe,
I see my deck, it's black
With one white stripe.

Still going fast,
I ollied too high,
Pulled a 1080° misty.
And flew into the sky.

I fell back down
And landed with a bump,
I felt my head
And there was a lump.

I got rushed to hospital
They put me in a bed
All I can say now is
I'm glad that I'm not dead!

Emily Lawrence (10)
Treliske School

MY PETS

Once I kept a sluggery,
The slugs were big and fat,
I didn't like it very much,
So I got rid of that.

I thought I'd run a snail farm,
I started the other day,
The snails were very slimy,
So I threw them all away.

Next I found a tadpole,
He turned into a toad,
He escaped and hopped away,
And got squashed on the road.

Then the centipede arrived,
He had a hundred legs,
It crawls along our washing-line,
Resting at the pegs.

The centipede got clean away,
So I bought in some ants,
You must be very careful,
They can get in your pants.

My ants live in an ant farm,
It's getting bigger by the minute,
But I'd be very happy
With more bugs to put in it.

Anna Ffrench-Constant (9)
Treliske School

THE STATUE

One night I went to get my homework,
I stood and stared at the bottom of the stairs.
I saw the statue creeping, creeping,
across the landing floor.
I heard his heart pounding,
his breath heaving,
as he moved across the landing floor
But then it began to creep back
And then in its old place and stood still as still,
My mum came out of the kitchen,
She got a teatowel and went back in the kitchen
it was as if the statue knew she was coming,
Then it crept to the top of the stairs,
It lifted its finger to its lips,
It said 'Don't tell a soul please don't tell,'
'I won't' I said. 'I won't.'
And it crept into my mum's room,
In the grim and gloom of the night.

Claire-Marie Goldsworthy (10)
Treloweth CP School

DEEP IN THE JUNGLE

Deep in the jungle where nobody goes
there's a big fat elephant washing his clothes,
With a ratatat here and a ratatat there
That's the way he washes his clothes.

Nicholas Wellstead (10)
Treloweth CP School

A Child's Prayer

A magical time
A new start.
Let us cancel all wars
Fill our hearts
Instead with new hope.
Let our future be bright
A true celebration
On millennium night.

Jesus was born to bring us great peace,
But we changed all that with lies and
deceit.
Two thousand years to get
the recipe right,
A feast of peace on millennium night.

Sally-Ann K Gretton (9)
Treloweth CP School

The Sea

The sea is a beautiful killer whale big and long
Its tail splashing on the ocean.
You could only see the black and white.
See it flipping in thy air
Its big long tail flapping in thy air
Its big mouth opening in thy air.
You could see it eating fish
But all you could only hear
is munch munch munch!

Richard Vicary (9)
Treloweth CP School

SUMMERTIME

I love summer when there are longer days
Because with my friends I can longer play
I can go to the beach and play in the sand
Which I do a lot with my Poppy and nan
We have barbecues on warm days when
My friends come to stay.
We have chicken, burgers and rice.
Which I think is really nice.
I wake up with a cheer
Six weeks off school this is really cool.
I make the most of its warm sun and
With my friends I have lots of fun
Around the corner winter waits with rain, wind
and banging gates.
Cheer up it won't be long
Before summer once again comes along.

Katie Armstrong-Smith (10)
Treloweth CP School

THE SKATEBOARD

Slip slide down the country lanes
You feel yourself in the breeze away from everyone
You are on your skateboard rolling down the beautiful country lanes.

Jonathan Ayres (9)
Treloweth CP School

YELLOW

I love the colour
yellow,
there are so many things
that are yellow
like butter, the sun
and the stars.

The colour yellow
is so
bright,
cheerful
and
strong
I just love the
colour
yellow.

Simon Pellow (9)
Treloweth CP School

THE SEA LION

The sea is a lion,
rolling on the beach all day
He is a nasty lion
he's big and fierce,
       With teeth like sharp knives
He bites the sandy shore.
       Where people are running round
having fun, what a peaceful sound.

Natalie Hole (10)
Treloweth CP School

RAINBOW

A rainbow is so colourful
it's like a ribbon you can pull
Red, yellow, pink and green
These are the colours that can be seen.

The rainbow is so beautiful
it arches like a waterfall
Orange, purple and blue
These are the colours of the rainbow too.

Karen Pascoe (10)
Treloweth CP School

VILLAGE LIFE

Young children playing, adults relaxing in the pub.
In summer people have picnics, animals run around in the woods.
Old people dancing in the village hall
People praying in the church.
Families on bike rides through the village.
Farmers going to market with their cattle.

Elliot James Bond (9)
Treloweth CP School

SUMMERTIME

Summer is a nice time of year,
People play on the beach all day,
And a nice warm breeze flows through the air,
The summer flowers are out in full bloom,
Children play outside in the sun.

Alaina Wheeler (10)
Treloweth CP School

THE WOODS!

As I walked along the gritty paths,
I hear the ripple of the water over the stream.
I hear the wind blowing through the trees above my head.
Crunchy leaves all around me, shrivel as I stand upon them.
Dogs barking echoing through the trees,
Squirrels scampering all around,
Fox in the woods hunting for its prey,
Birds jabbering to each other,
Flock and run for cover.
Bike wheels squeaking,
People's feet upon the rotted old worn out path.

Liam Thomas (10)
Treloweth CP School

THE SEA

The sea is a roaring lion, and the lion
crashes against the cliffs, and the lion has
great big paws like a giant's hand, and the
lion is a shape of a whale and is like big
fireballs, and he crashes the rocks with his
head and makes the cliffs shake and wobble,
and teeth like great giant metal bars and a
tongue like a giant octopus's leg.

Nathan Vinnicombe (10)
Treloweth CP School

THE SEA

The sea is an old seal
grey and soft.
Moving slow but gently
on one summer's day.
The noise of the waves
are his flaps in the water,
and his giant tail moves with
the splash, splash, splash.
In the night the wind roars,
Just about to go to sleep
When the lighting wakes him
Up, but he licks his paws
and goes back to sleep.

Jody Long (10)
Treloweth CP School

MILLENNIUM

There's going to be a party
People with happiness and good cheer
The party is for the millennium
To bring us into a New Year.

So come on celebrate!

There'll be people singing
and also dancing.
Everyone will be quite merry
Especially when the fireworks go
ohhhm bang.

So come on celebrate!

Daniel Devey (10)
Treloweth CP School